I0446978

THANK YOU FOR YOUR PURCHASE!
IF YOU ARE SATISFIED WITH YOUR
PURCHASE, PLEASE CONSIDER LEAVING A
REVIEW. IT TAKES 5 SECONDS AND GREATLY
HELPS OUT SMALL BUSNINESSES LIKE OURS.

Color Test Page

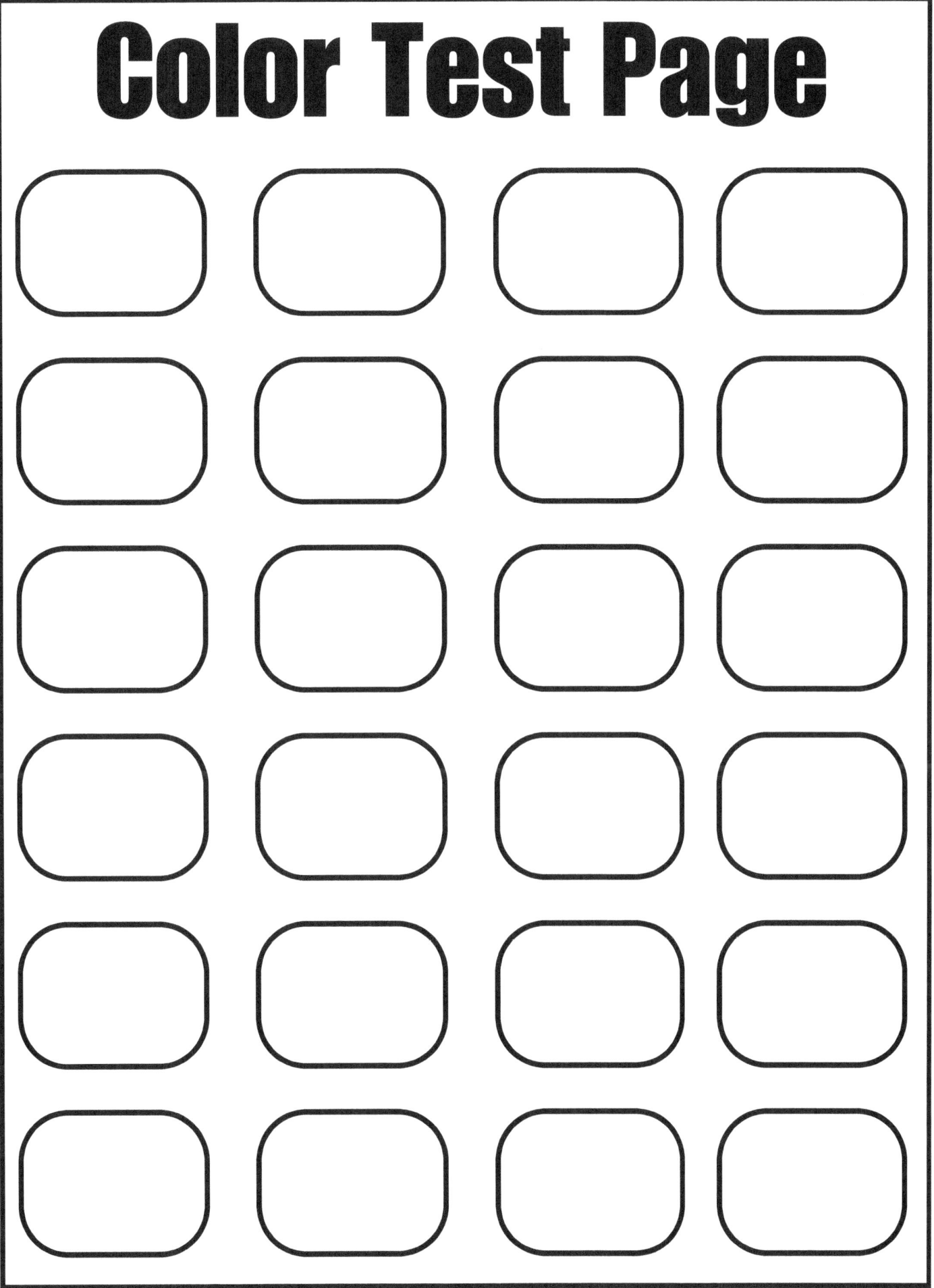

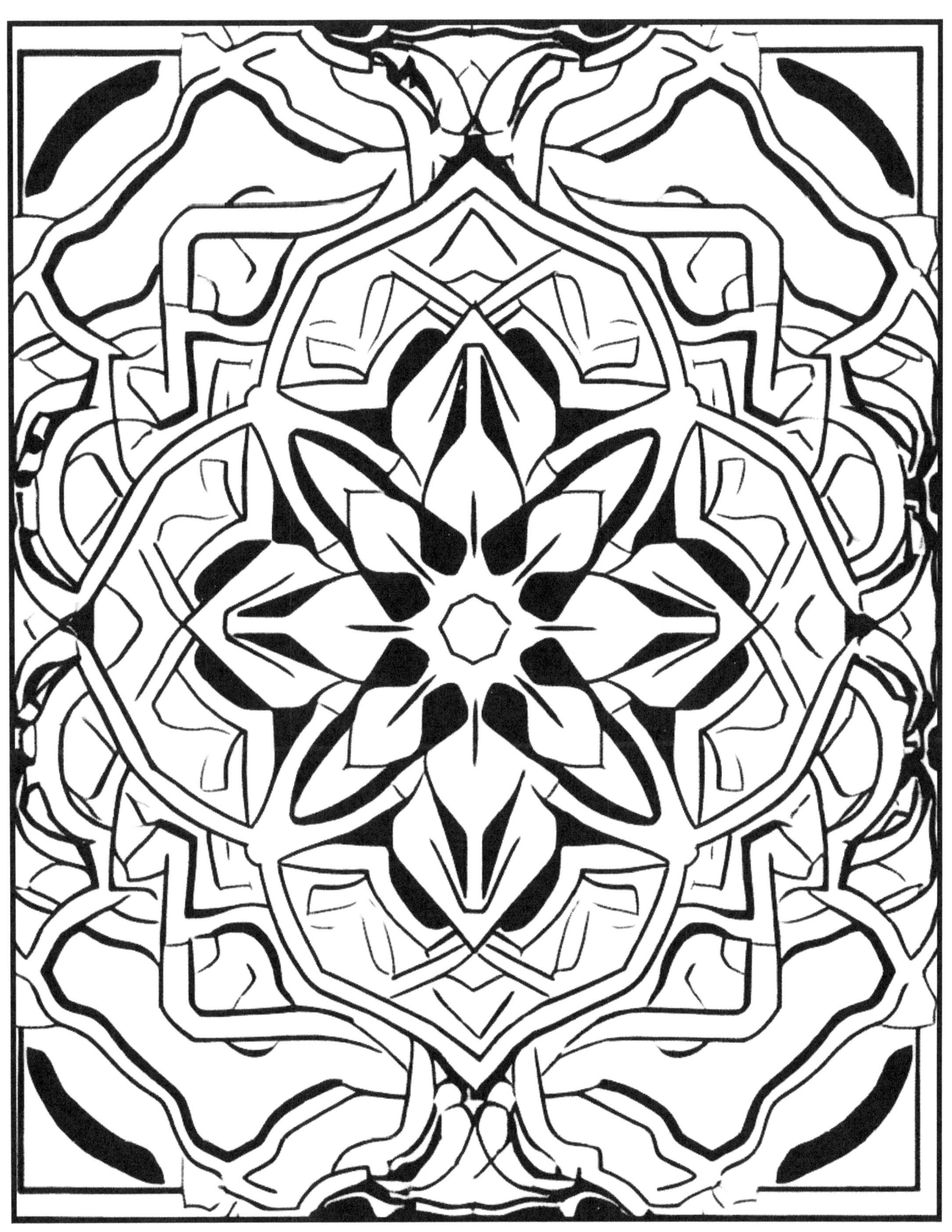

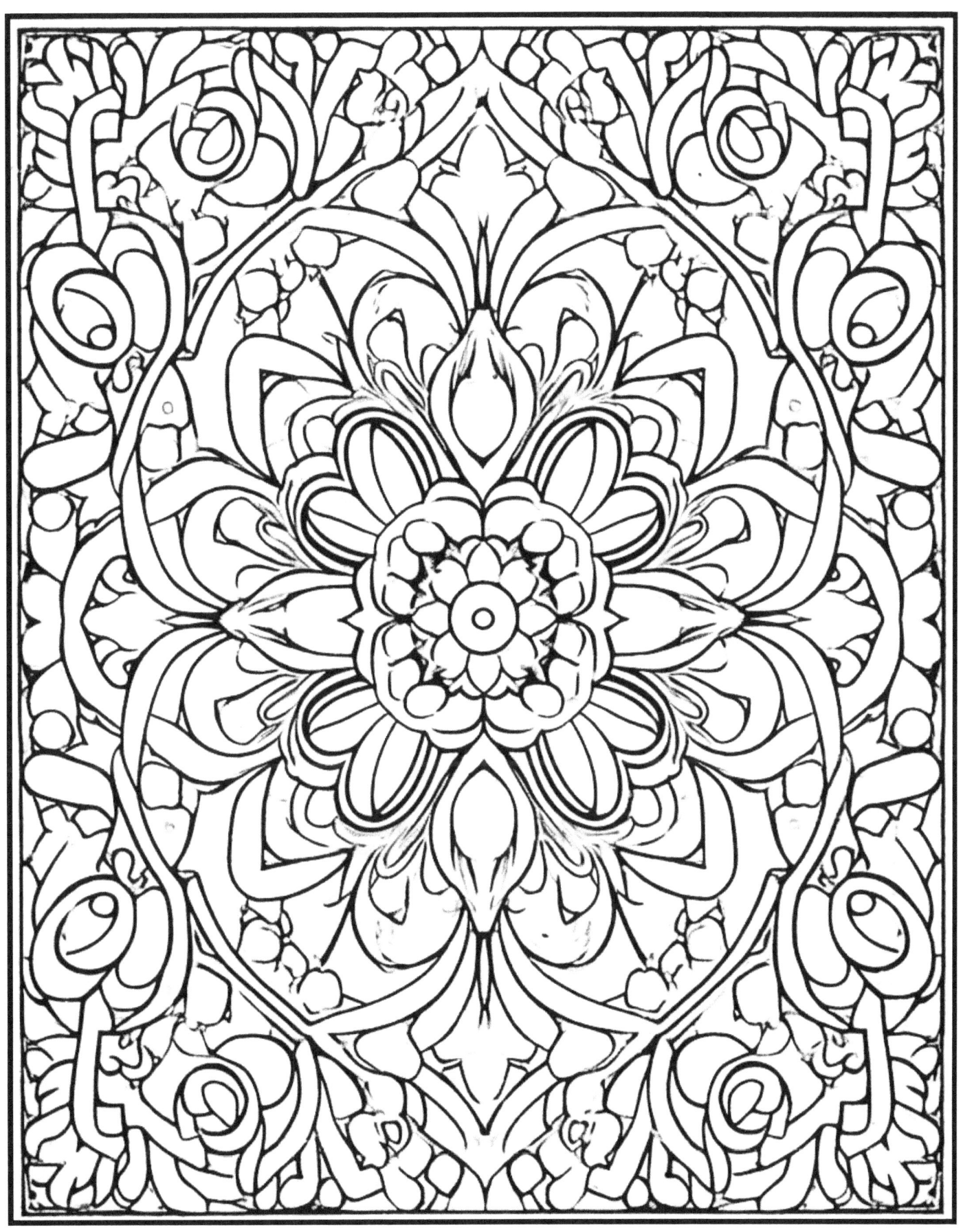

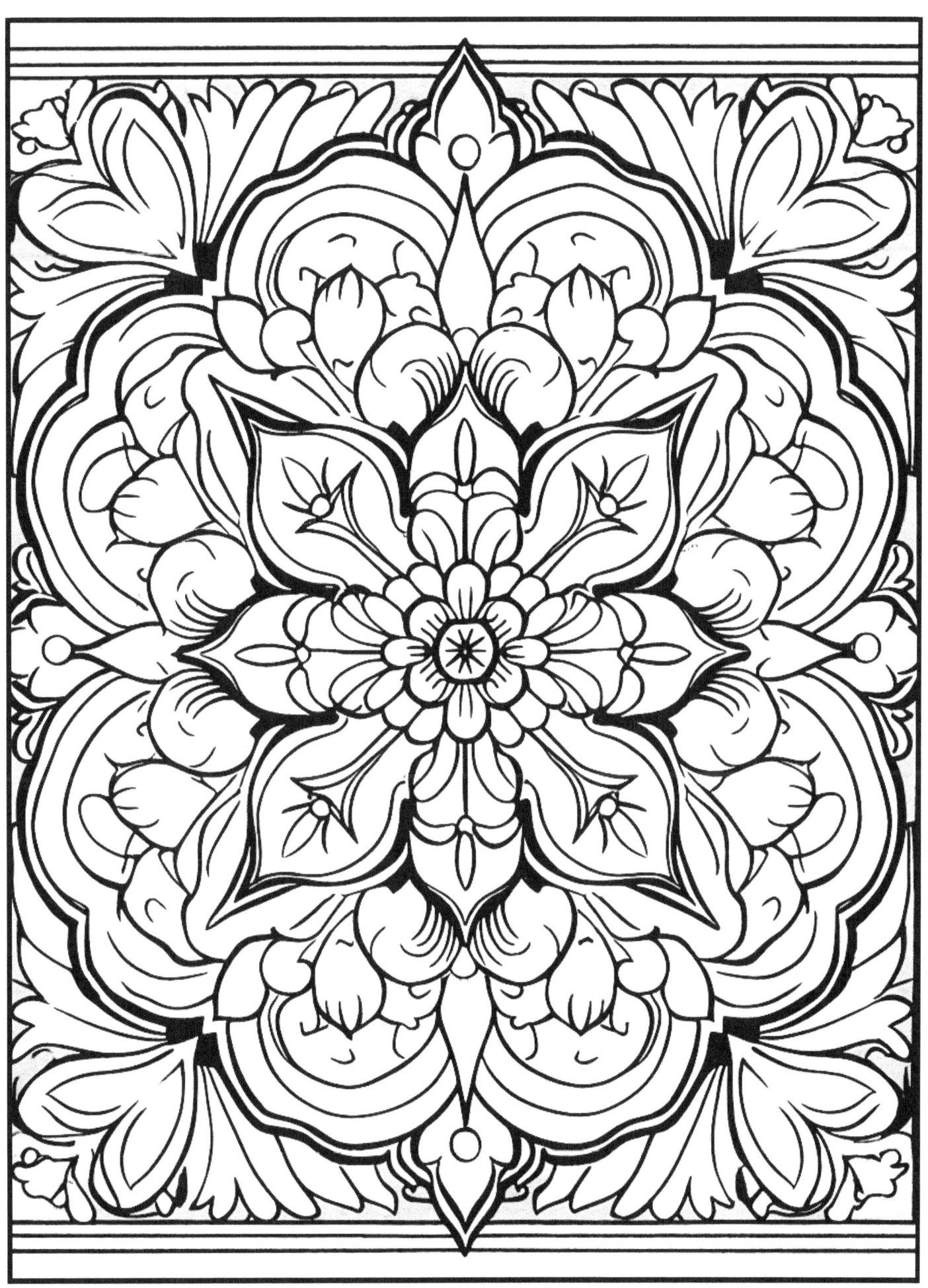

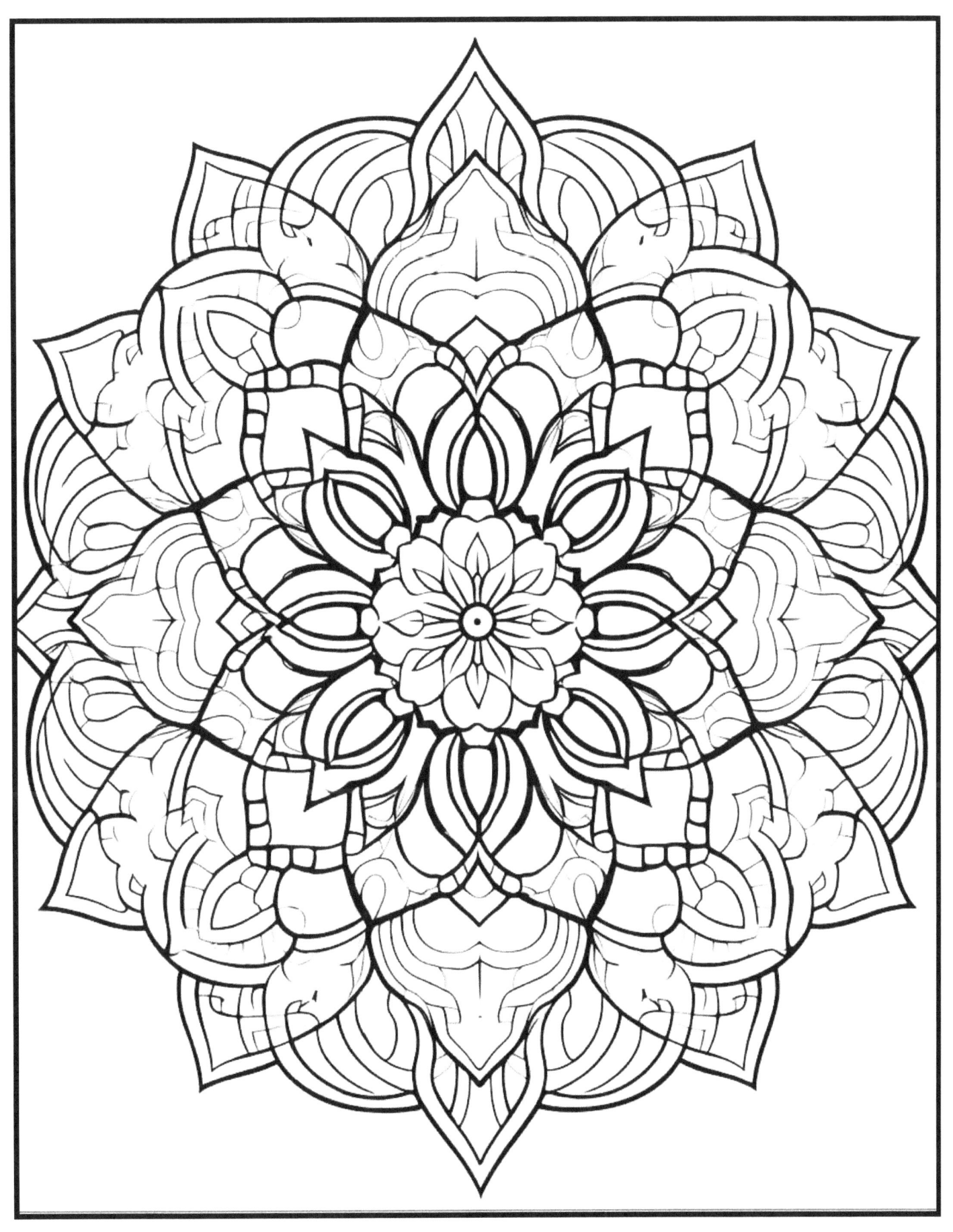

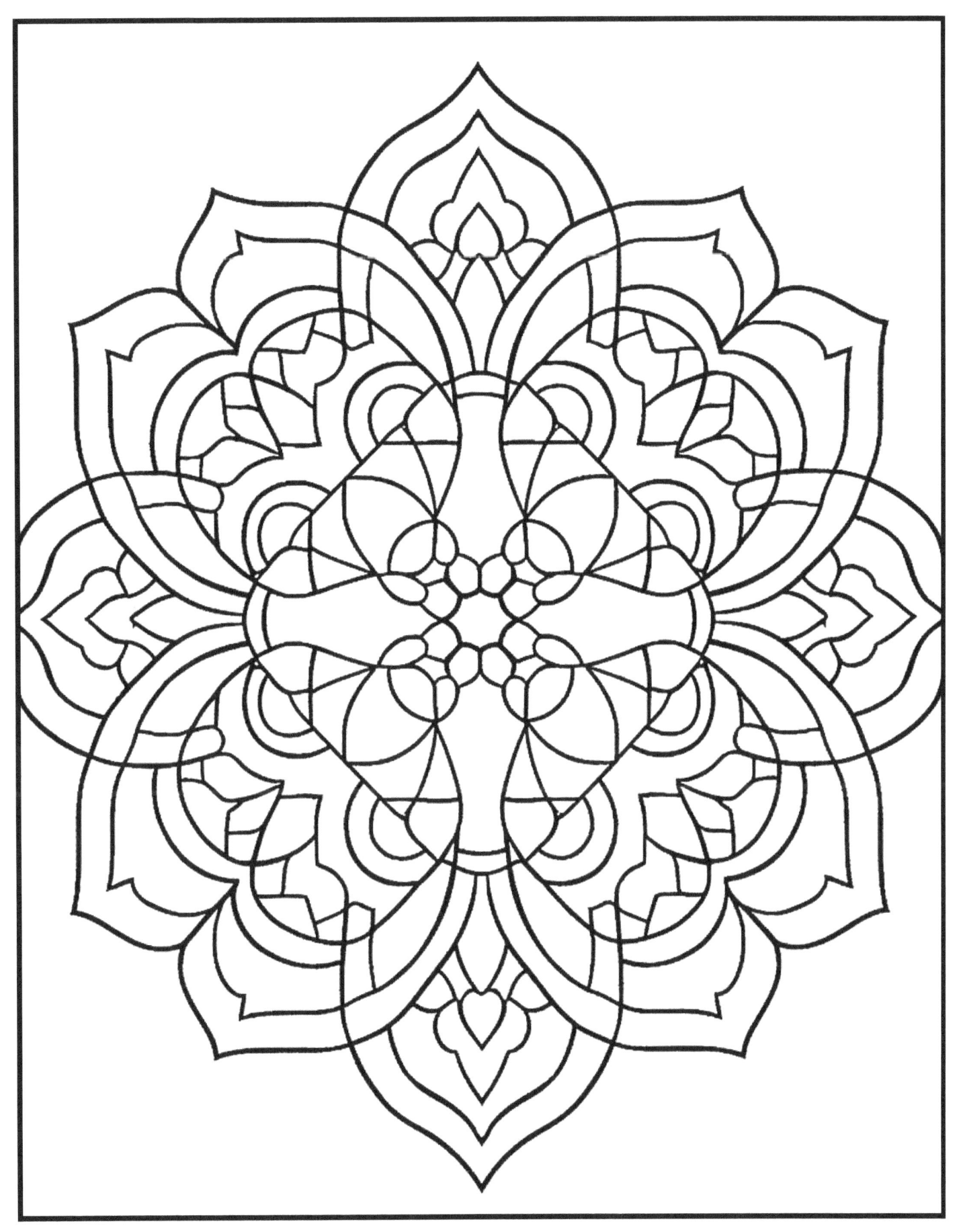

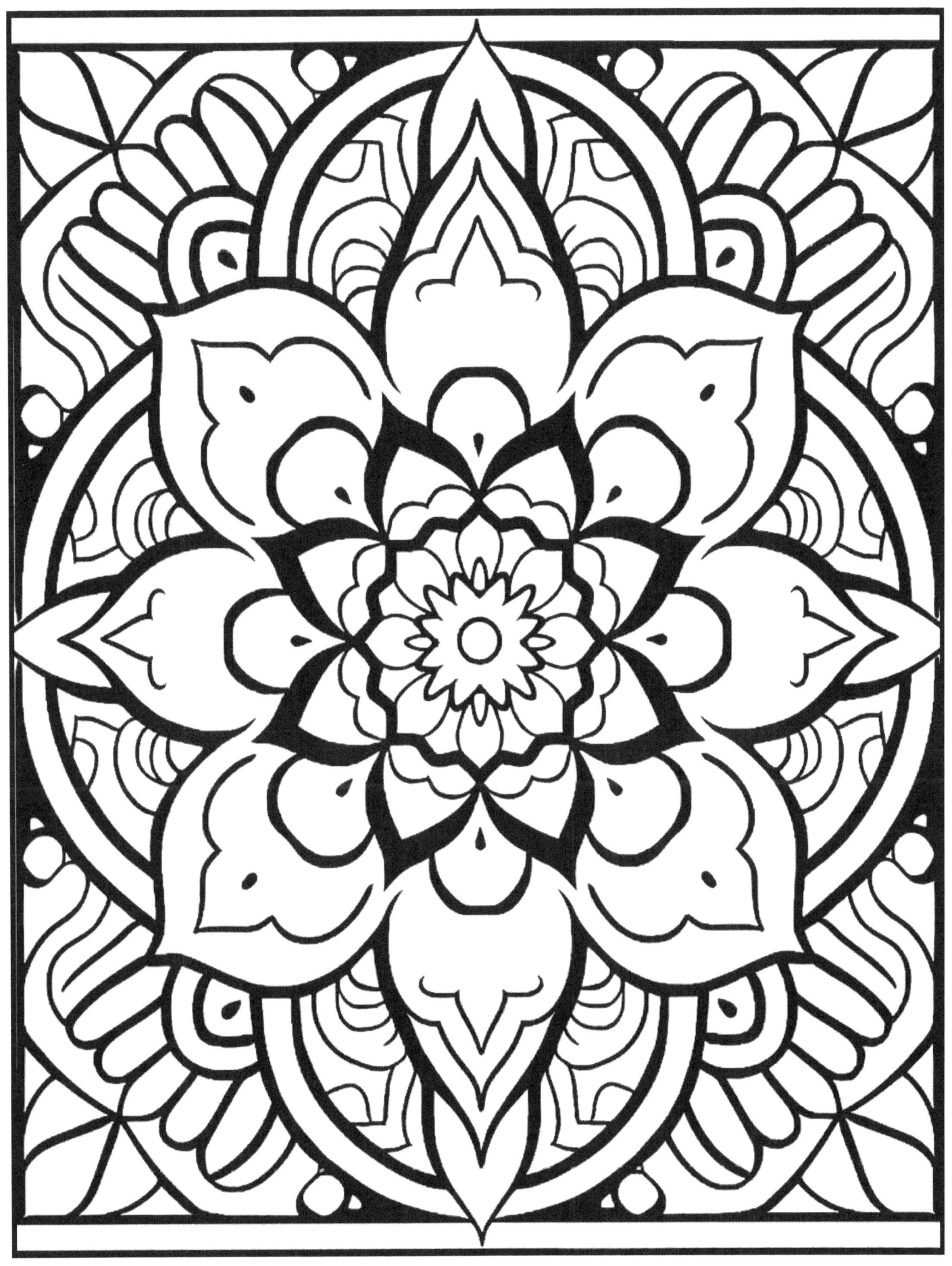

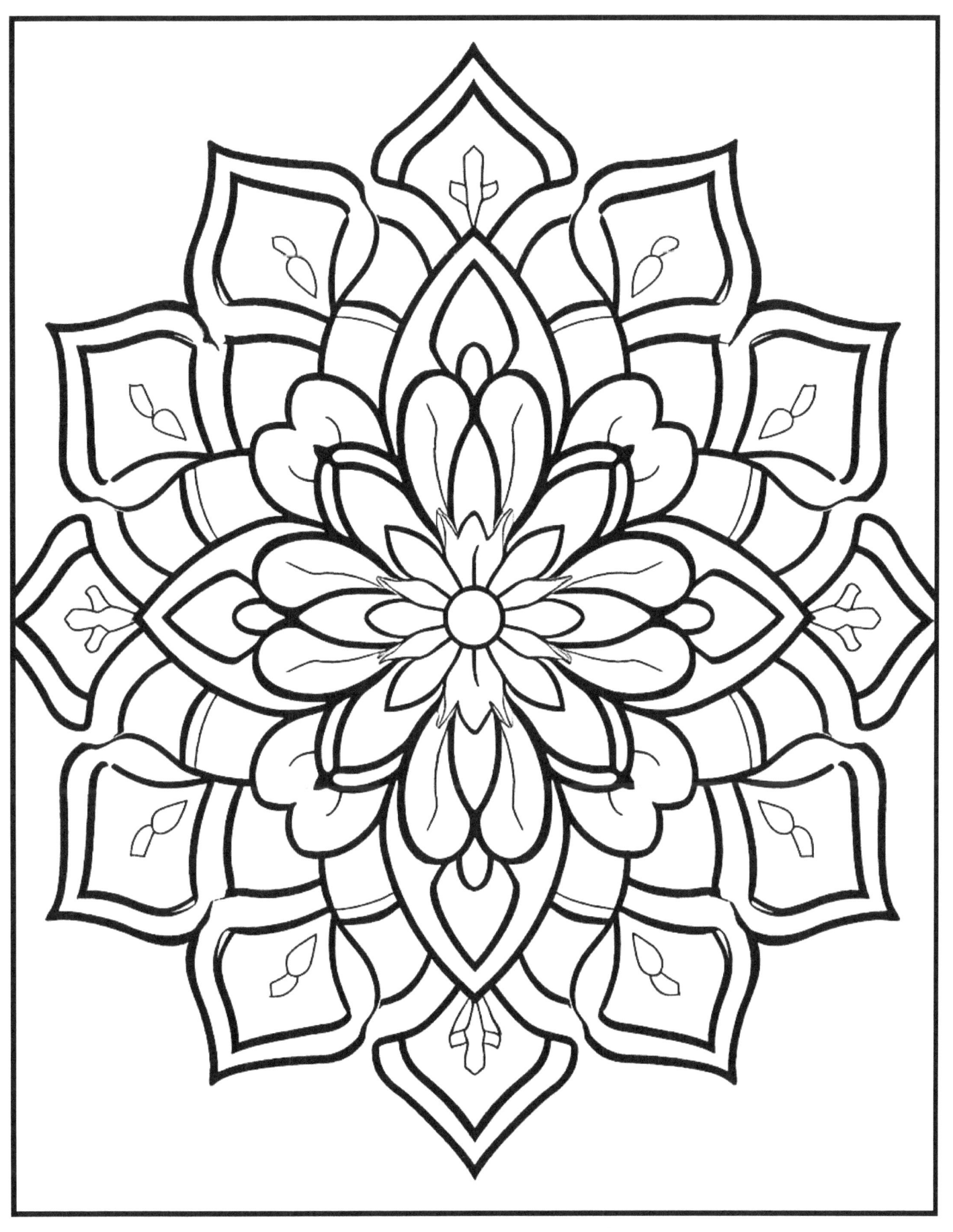

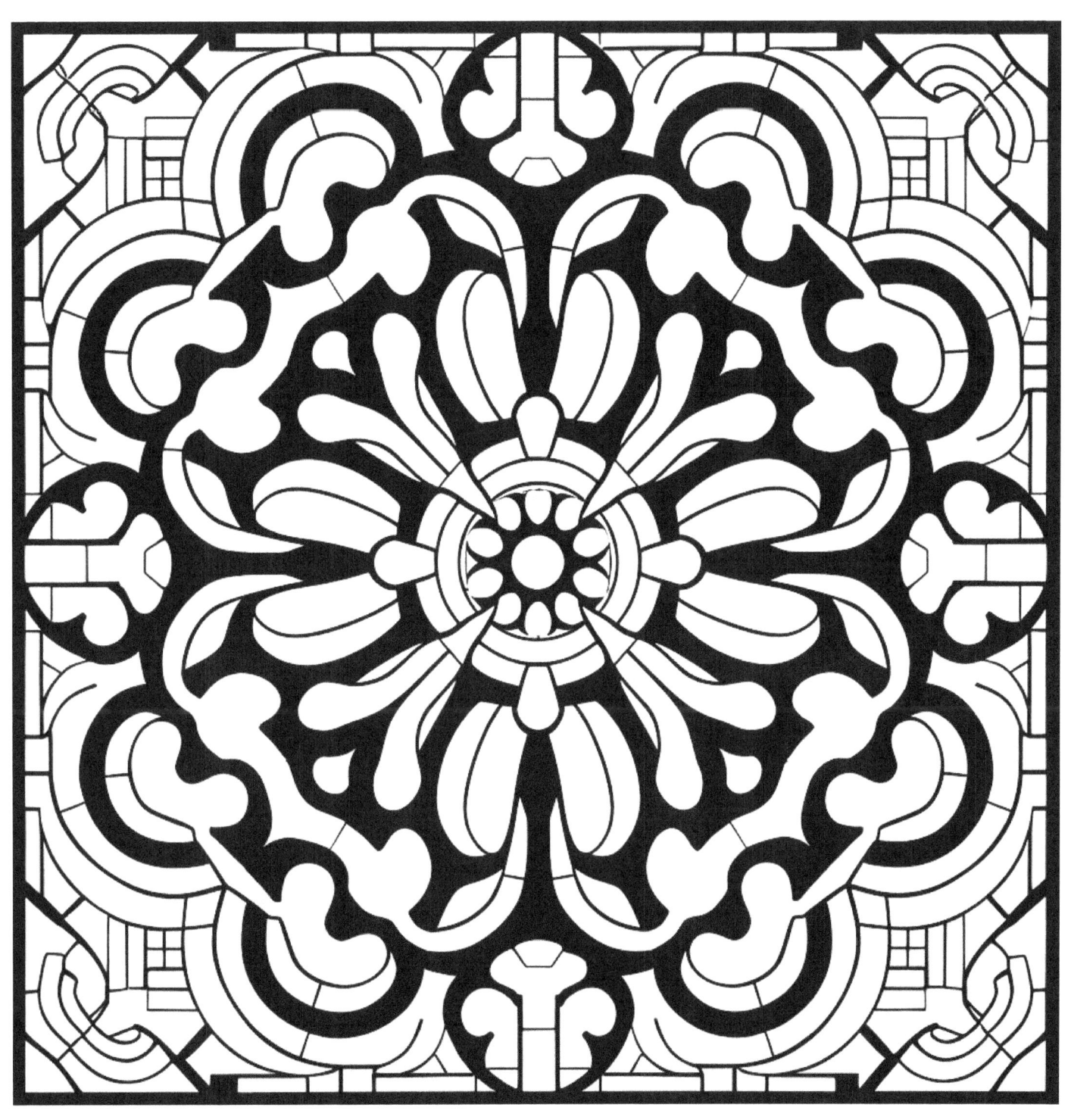

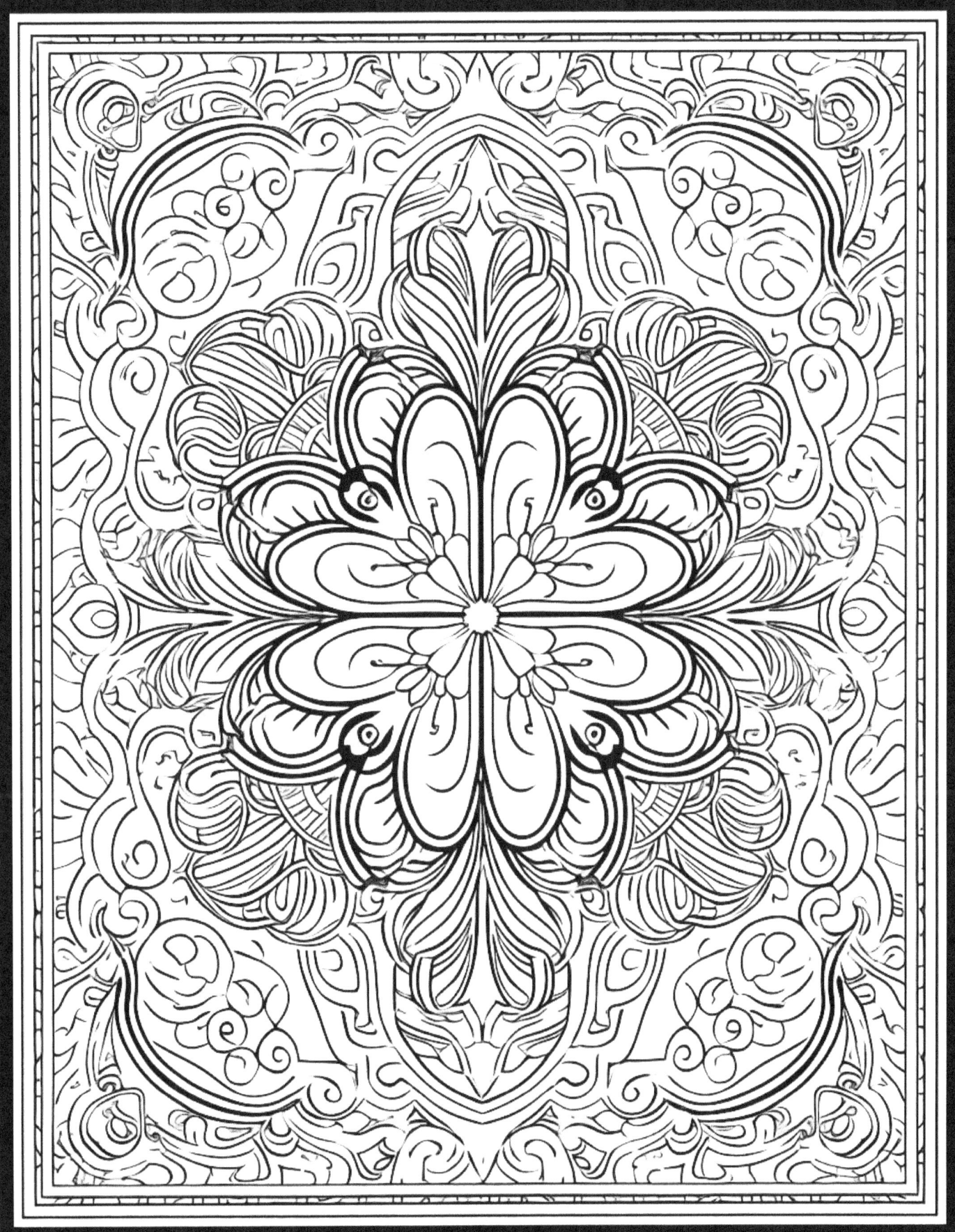

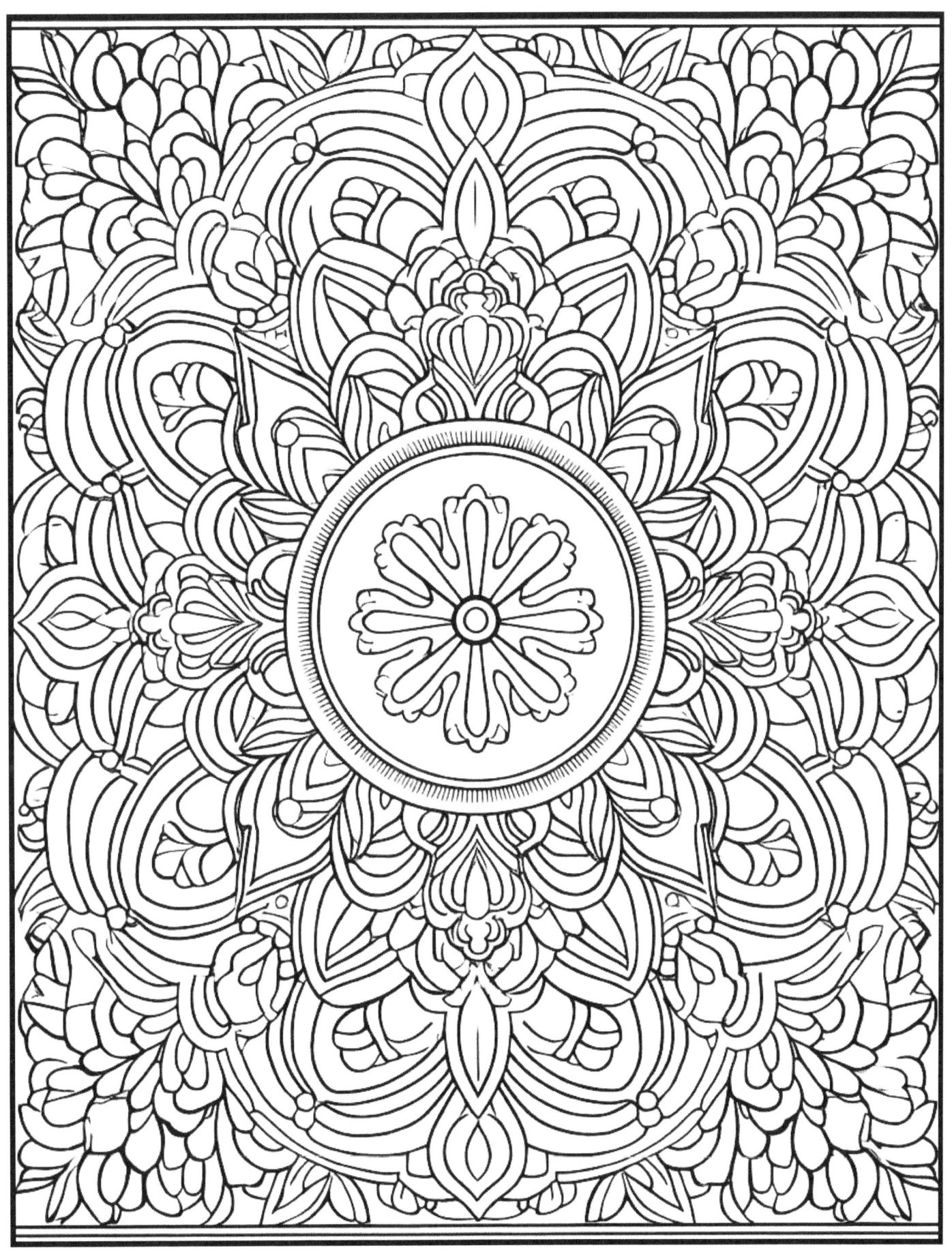

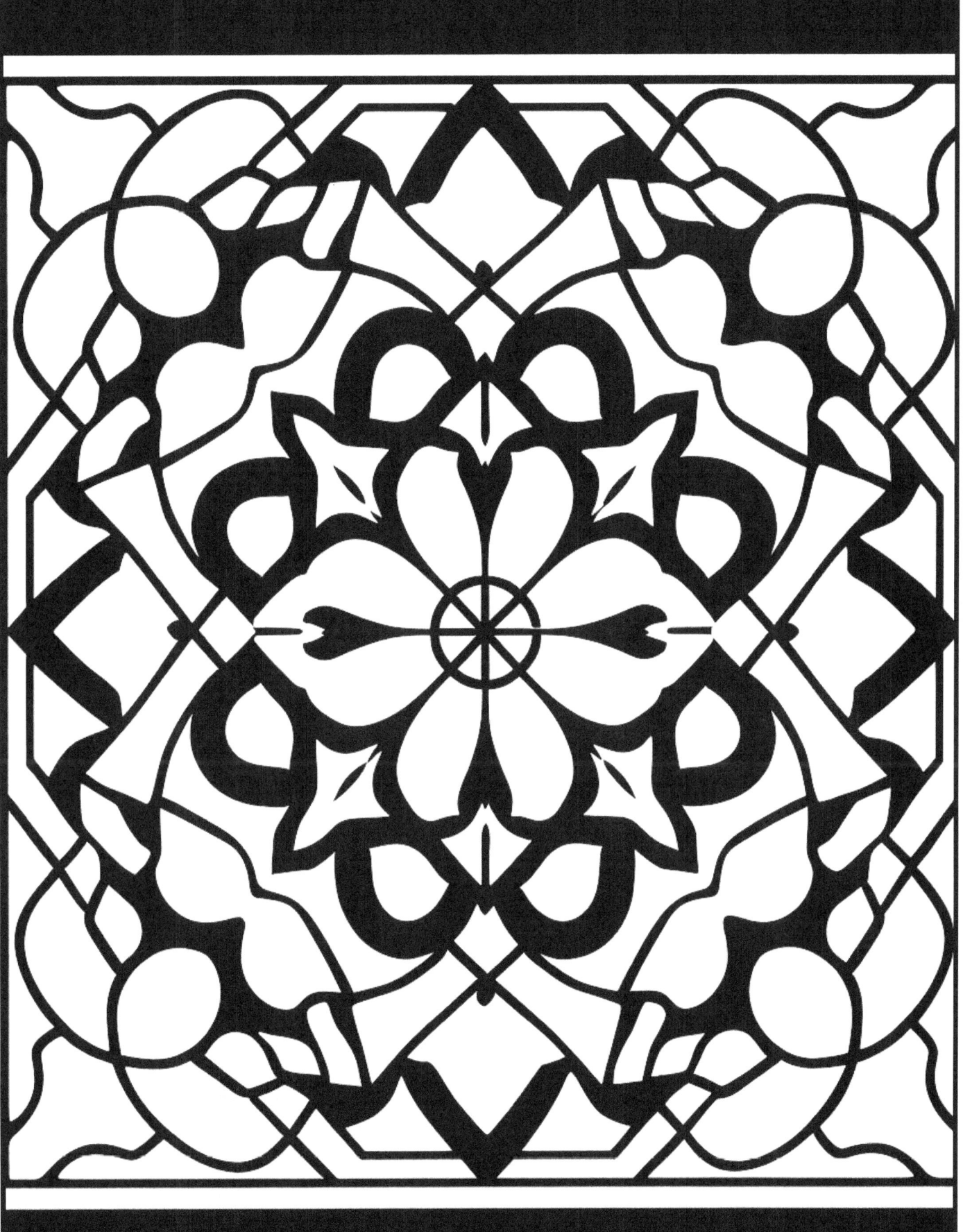

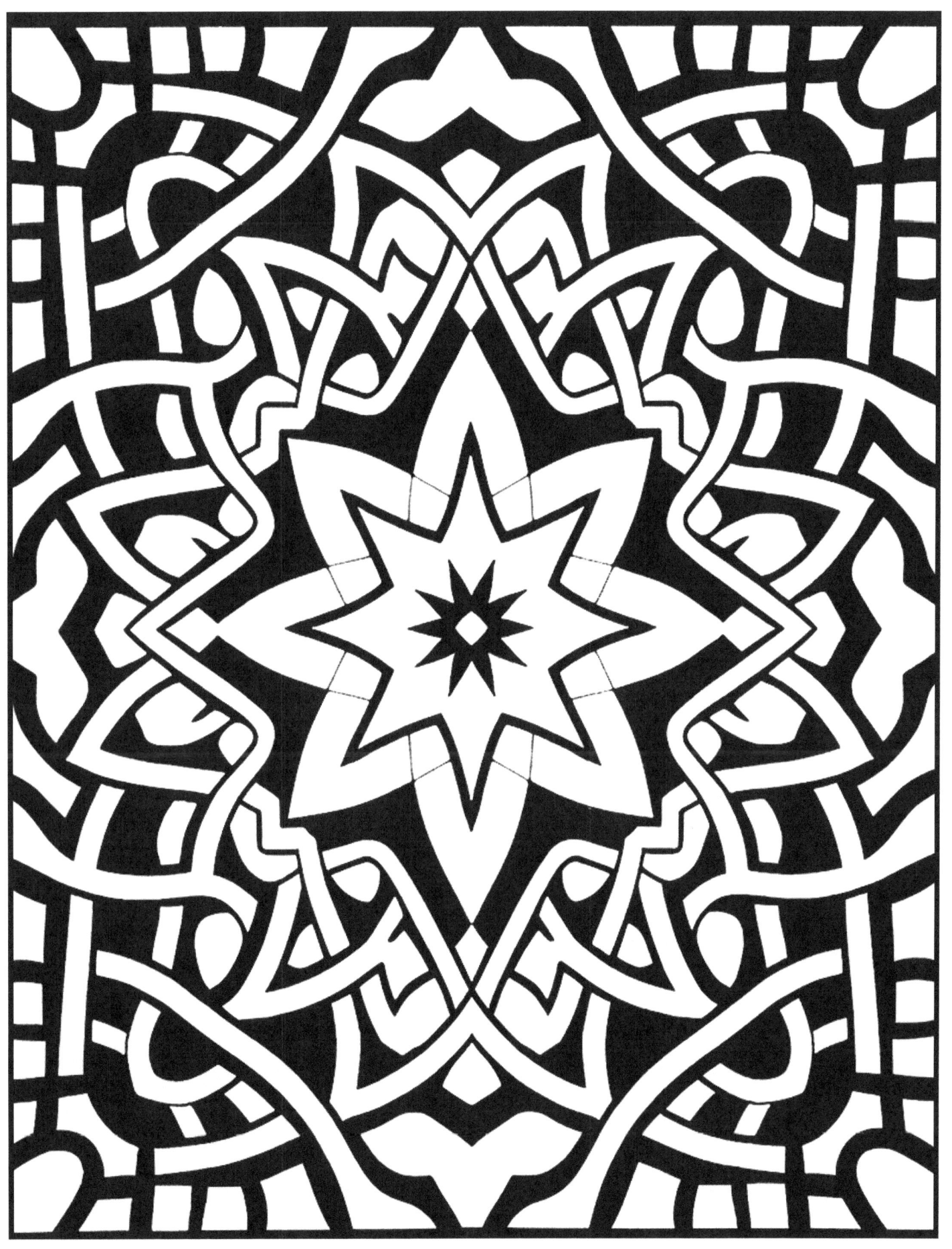

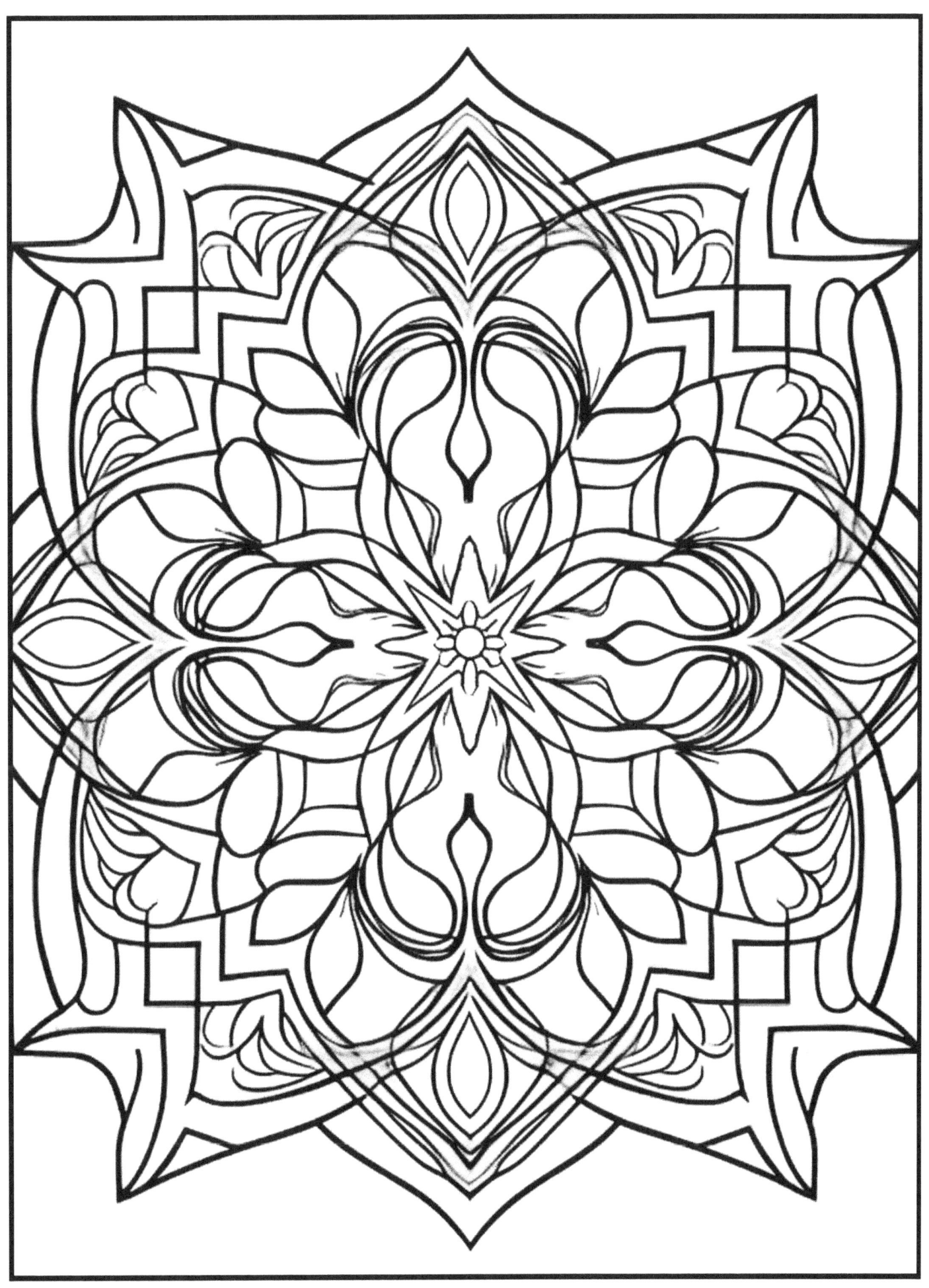

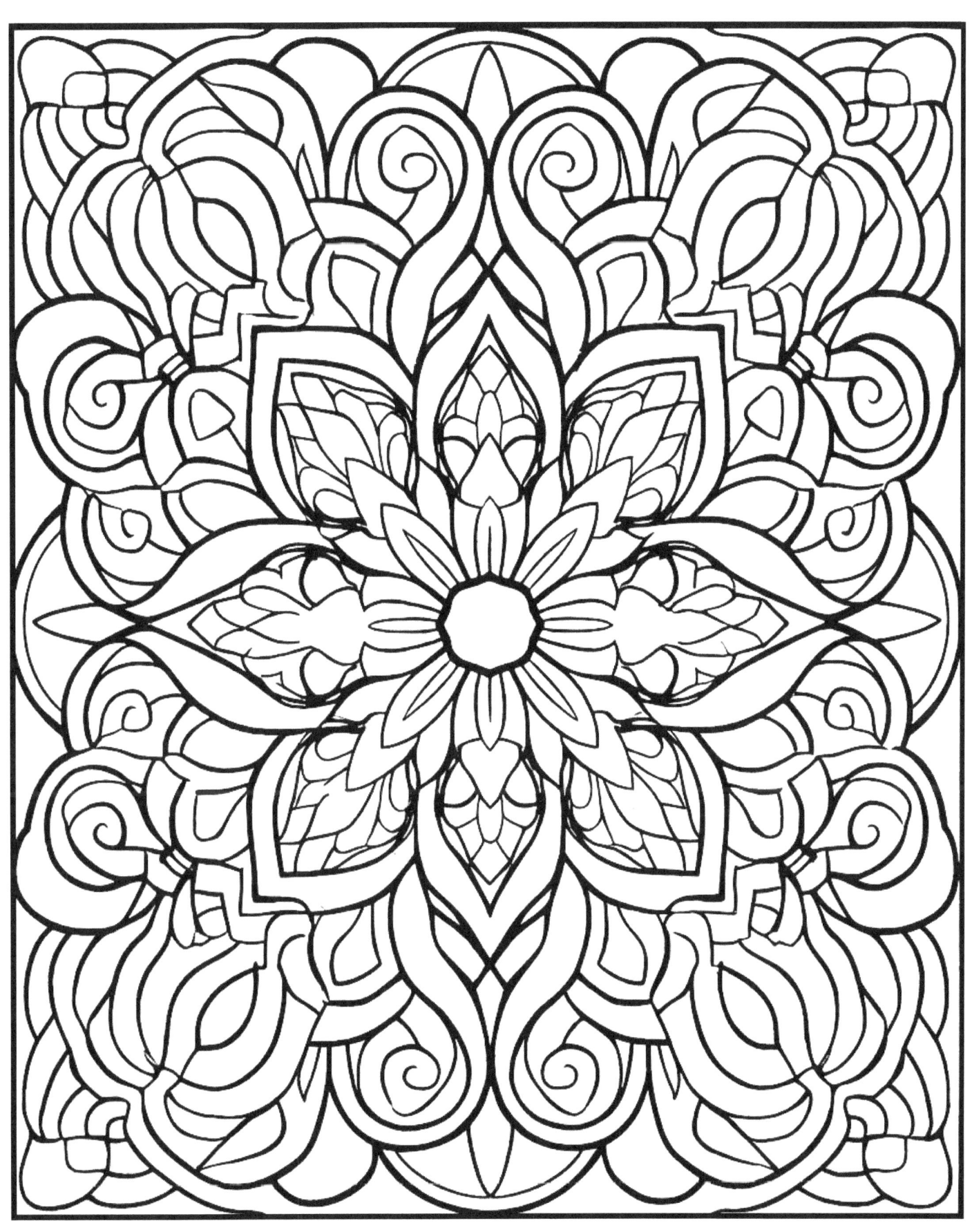

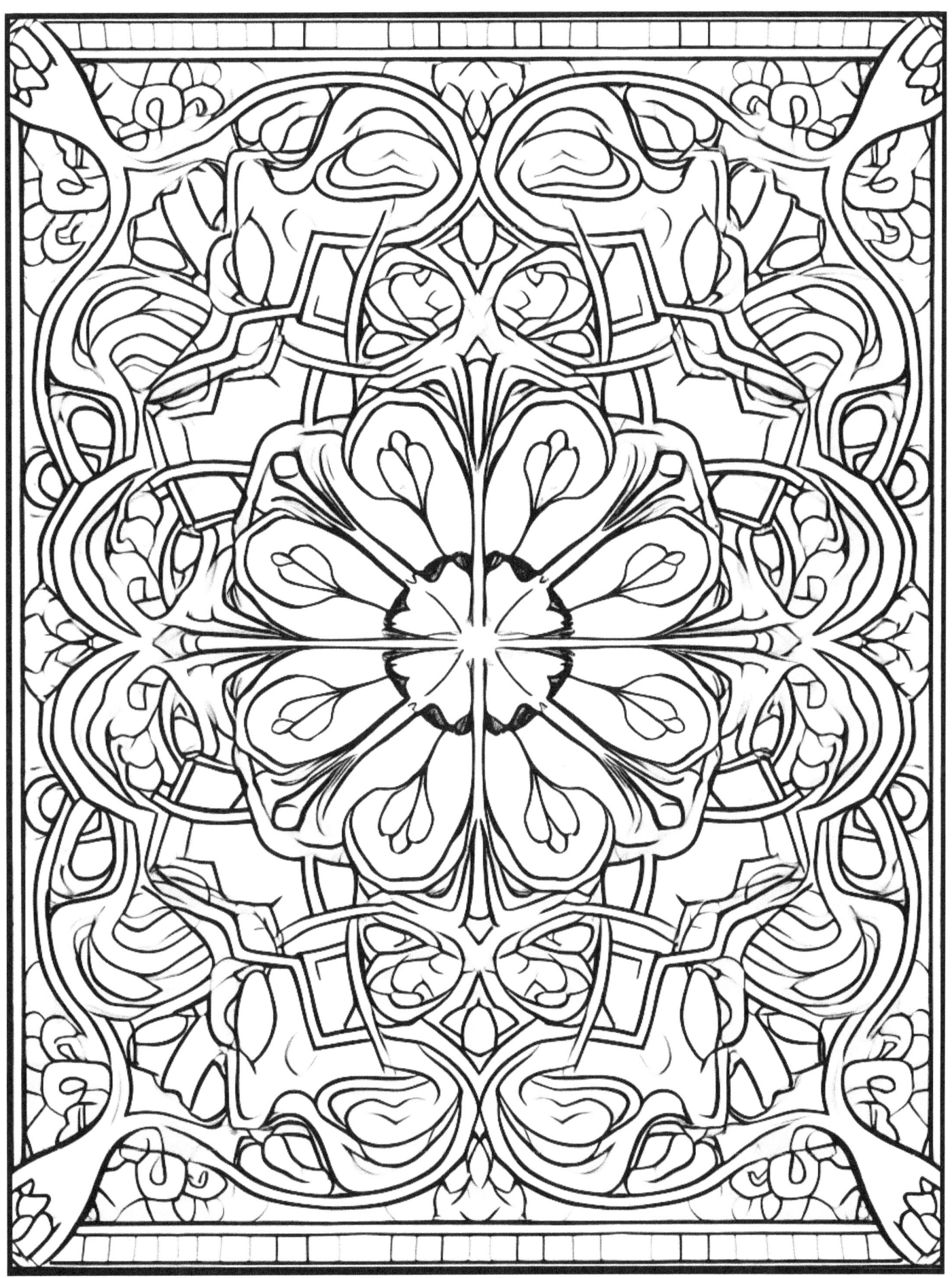

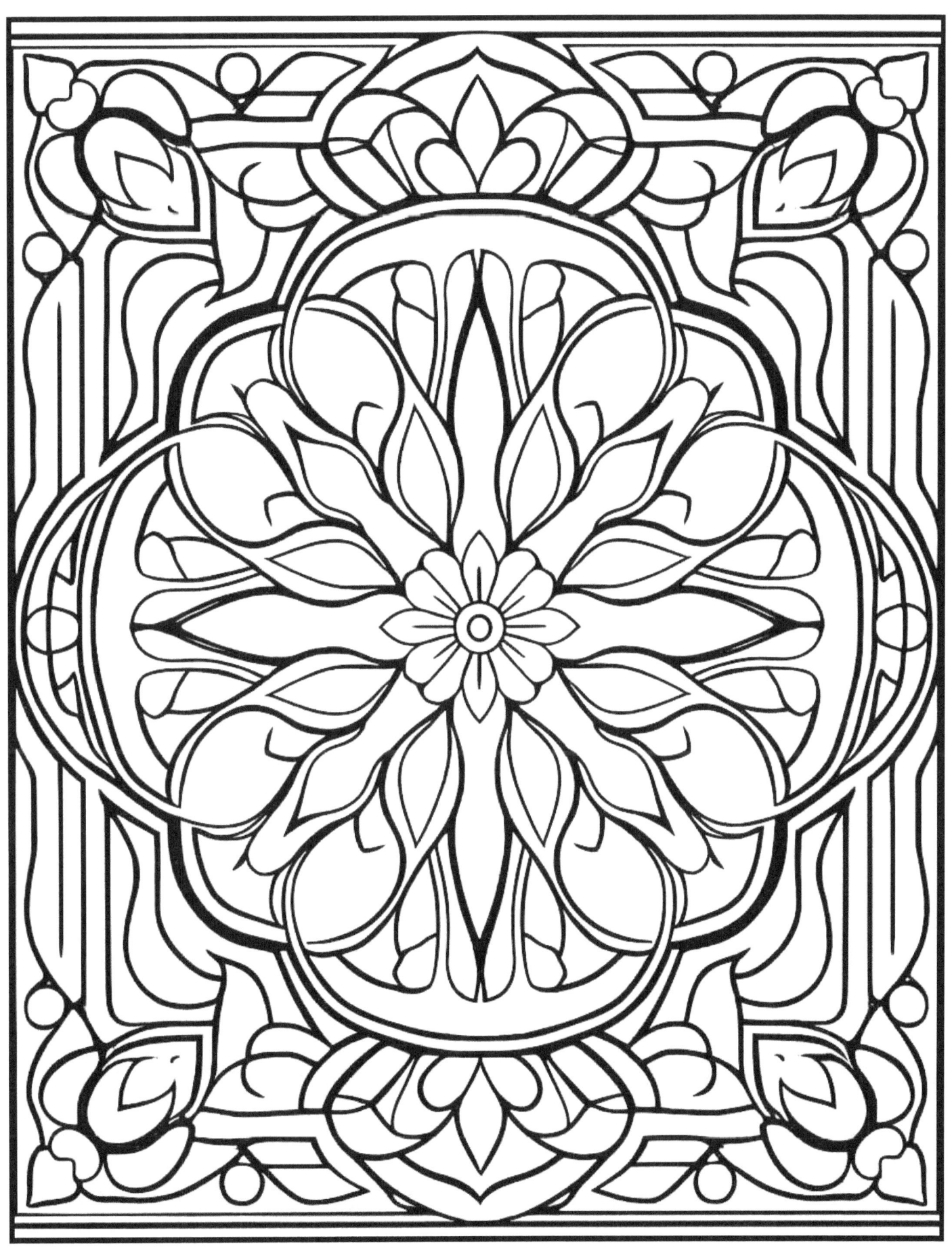

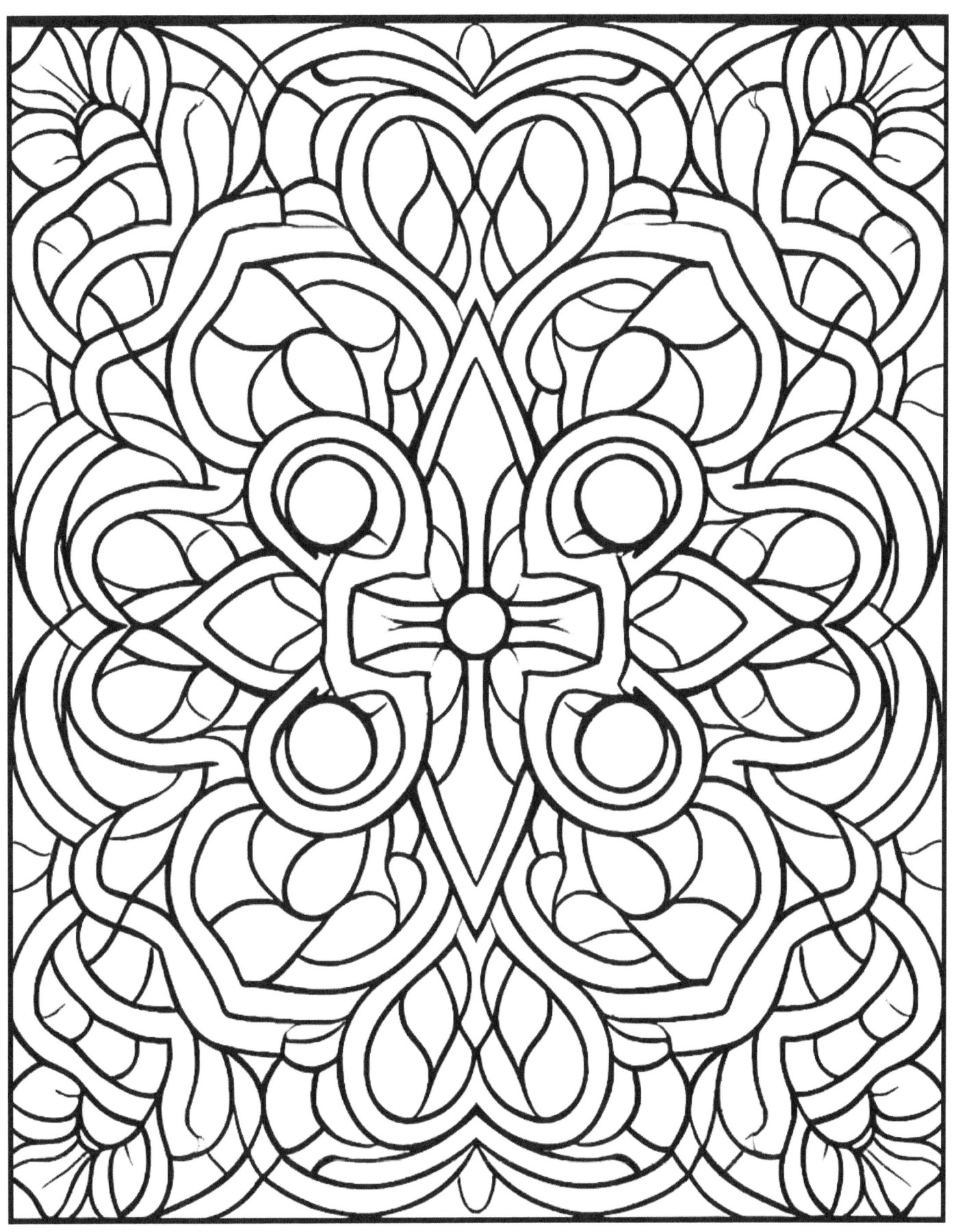

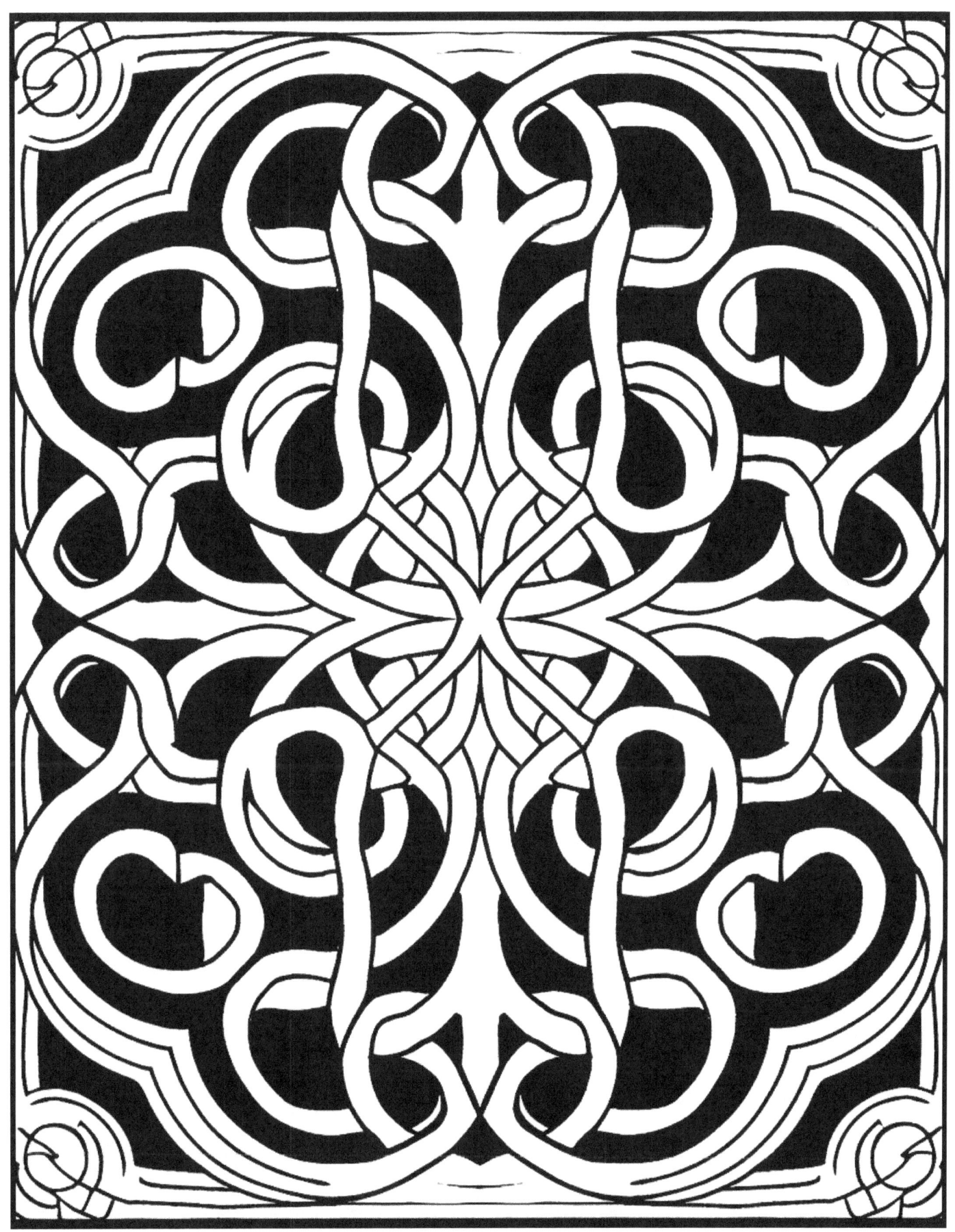

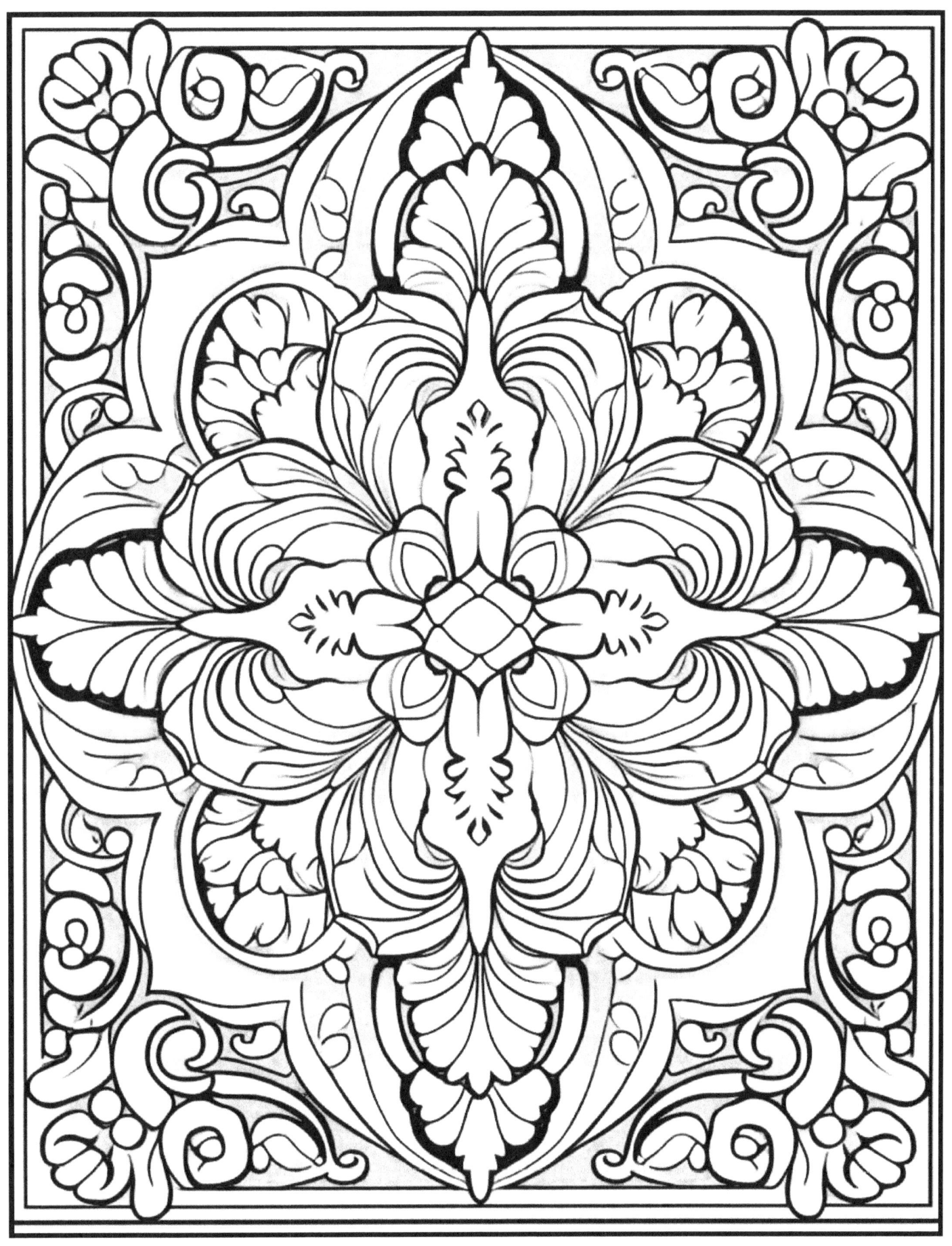

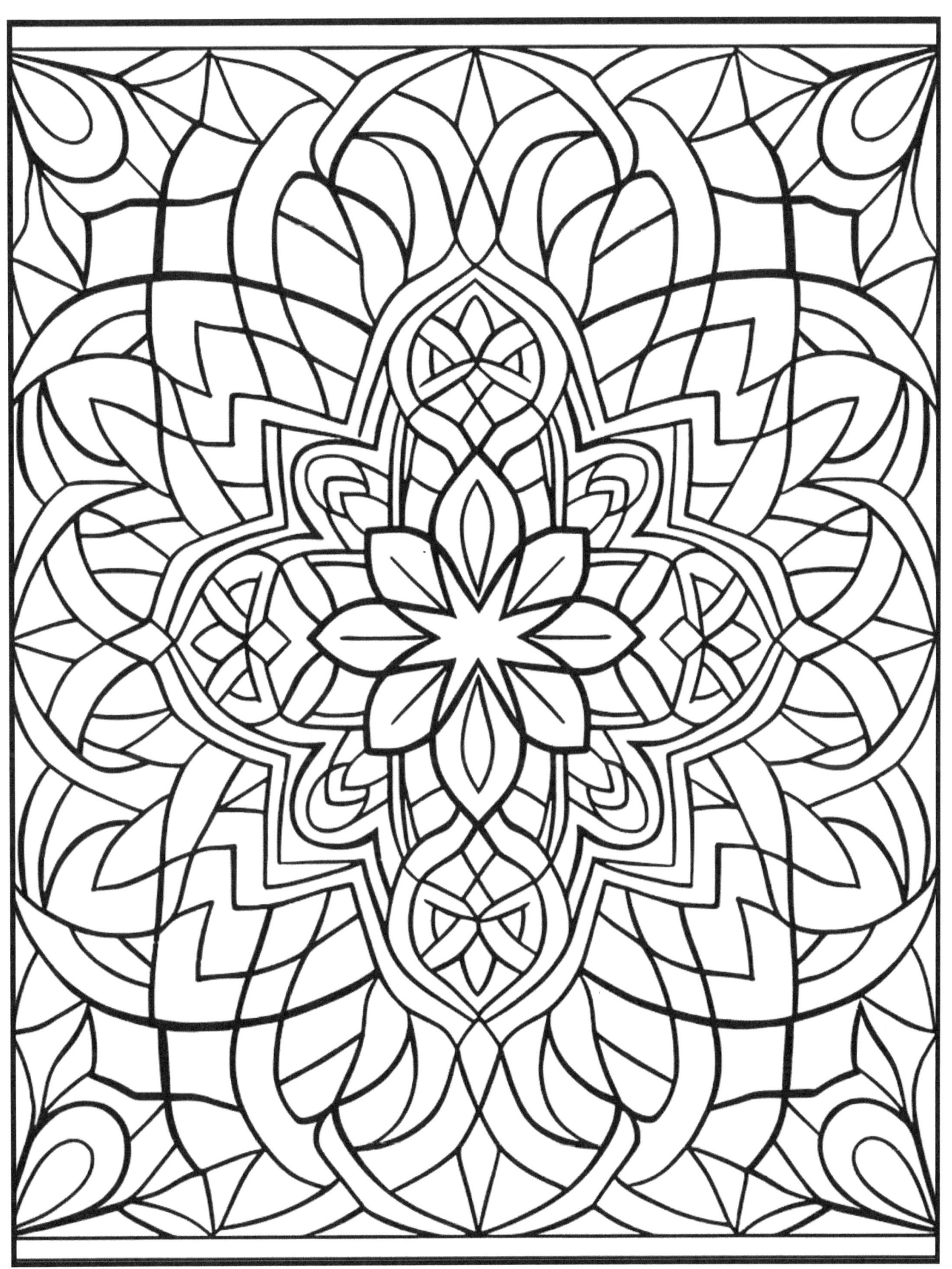

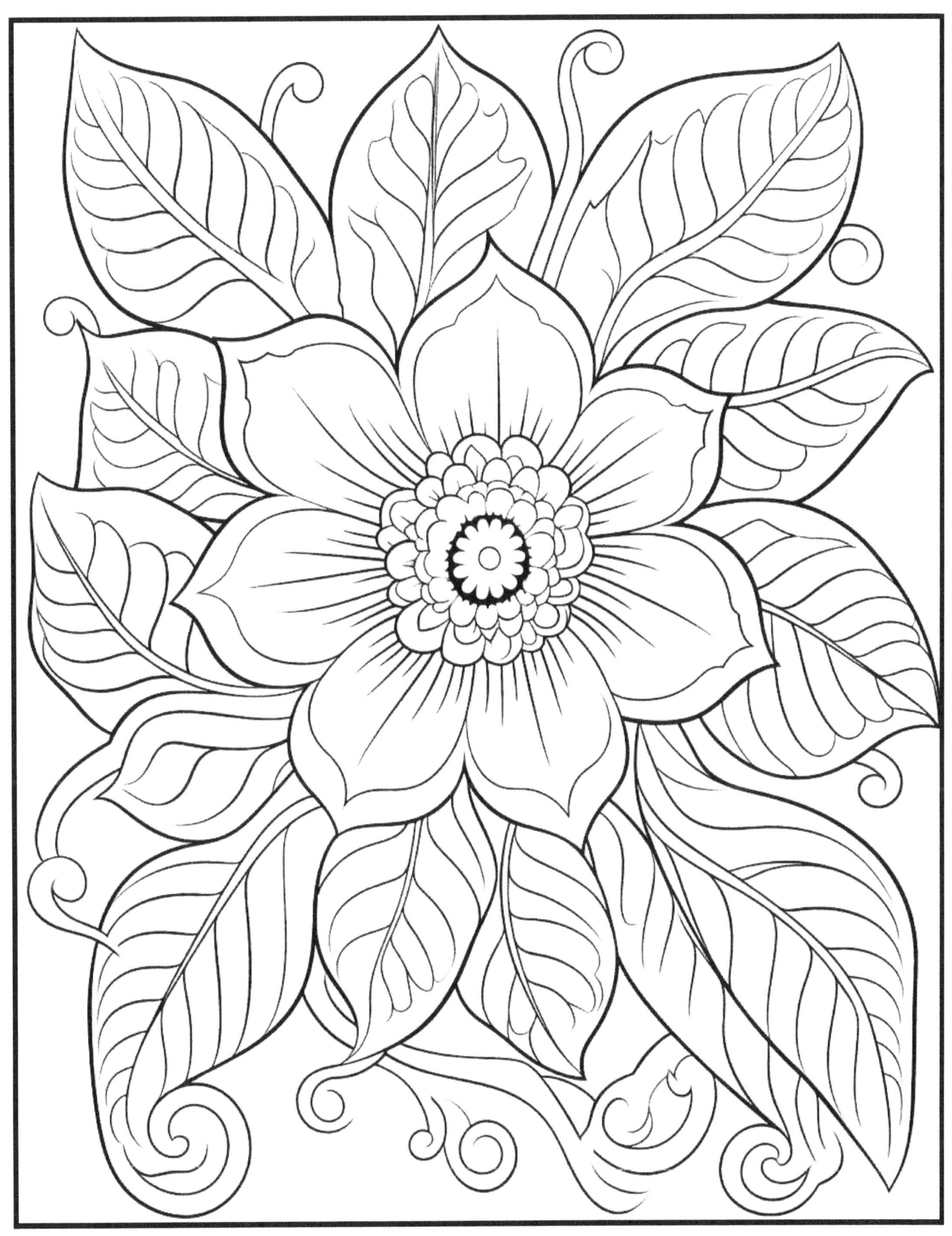

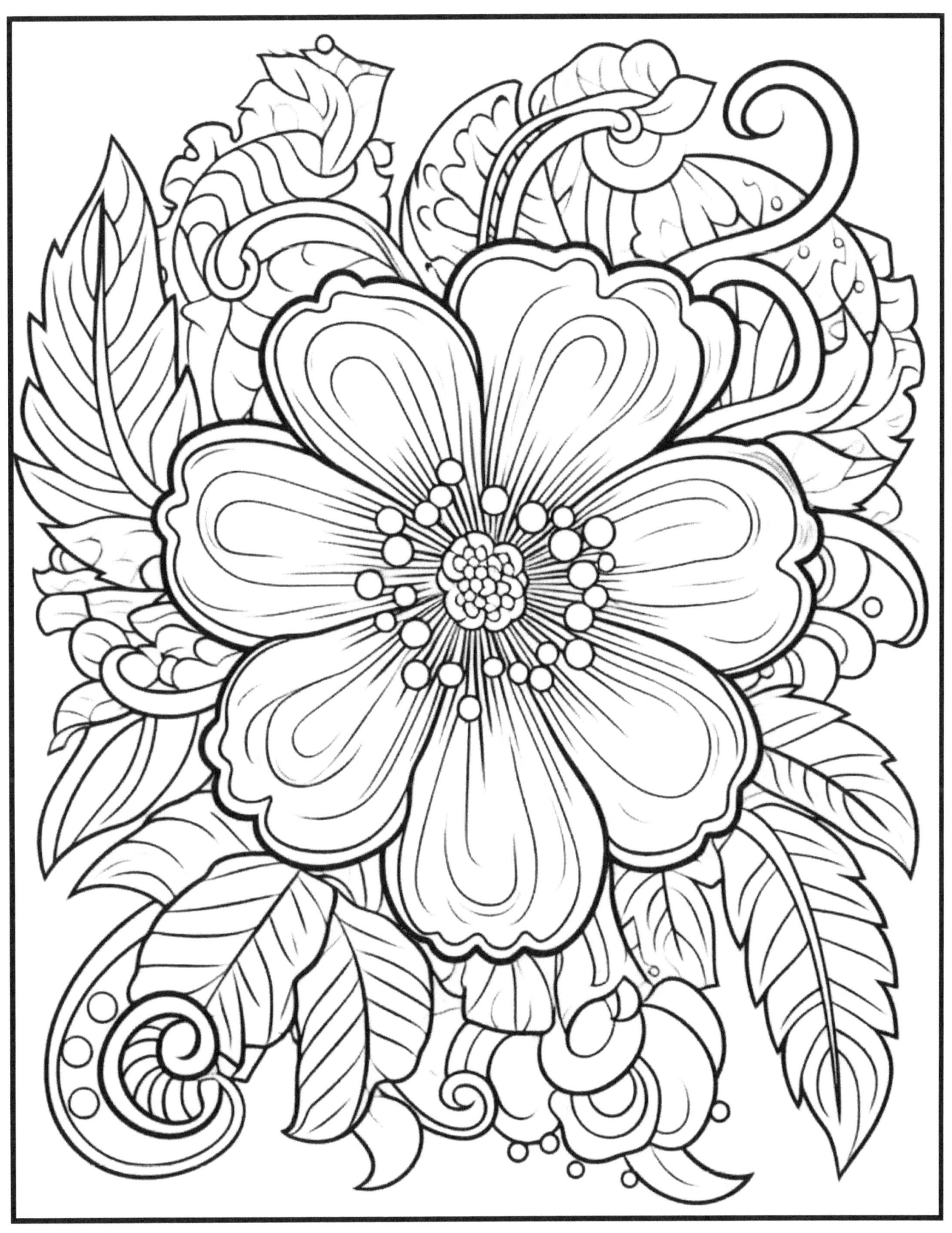

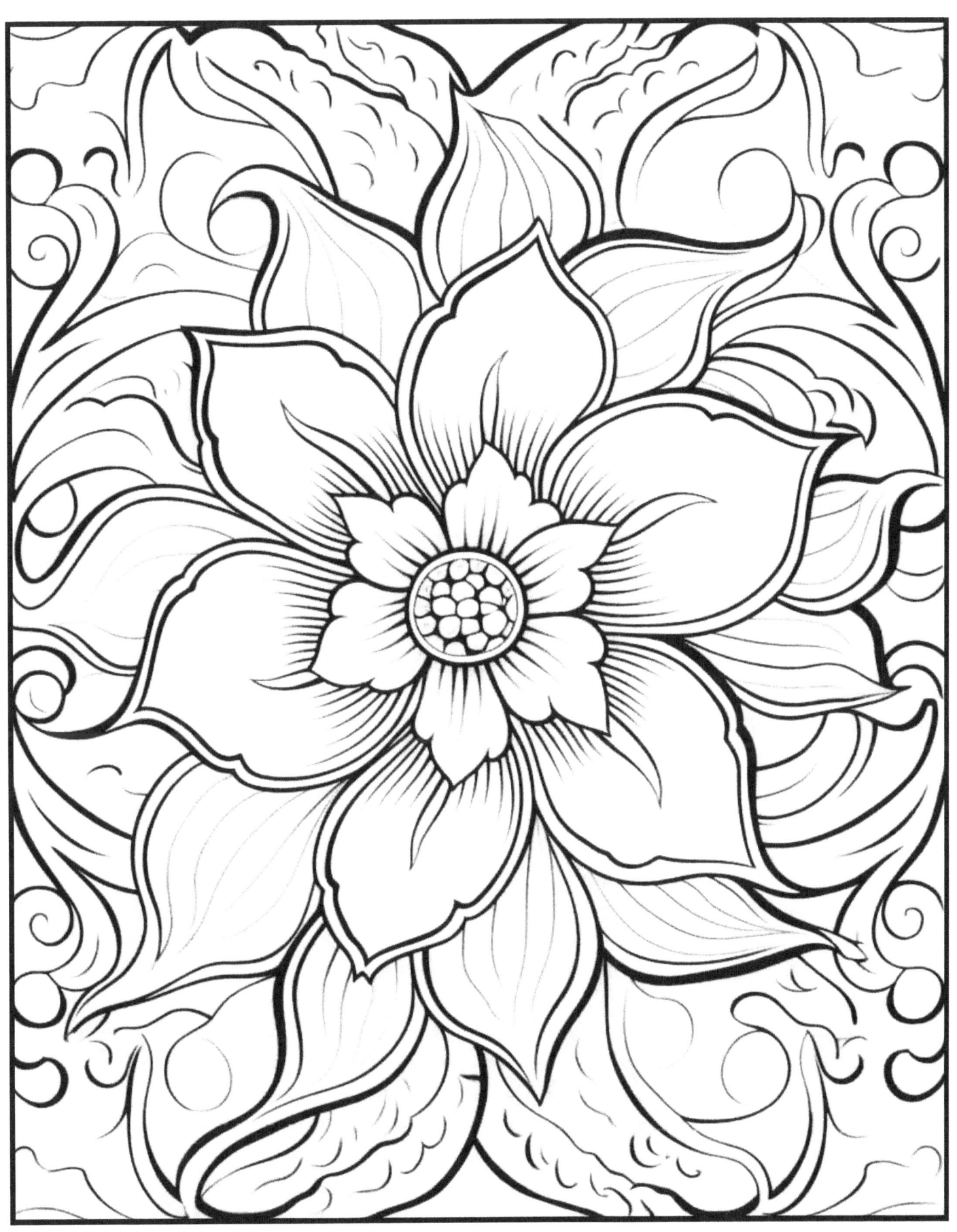

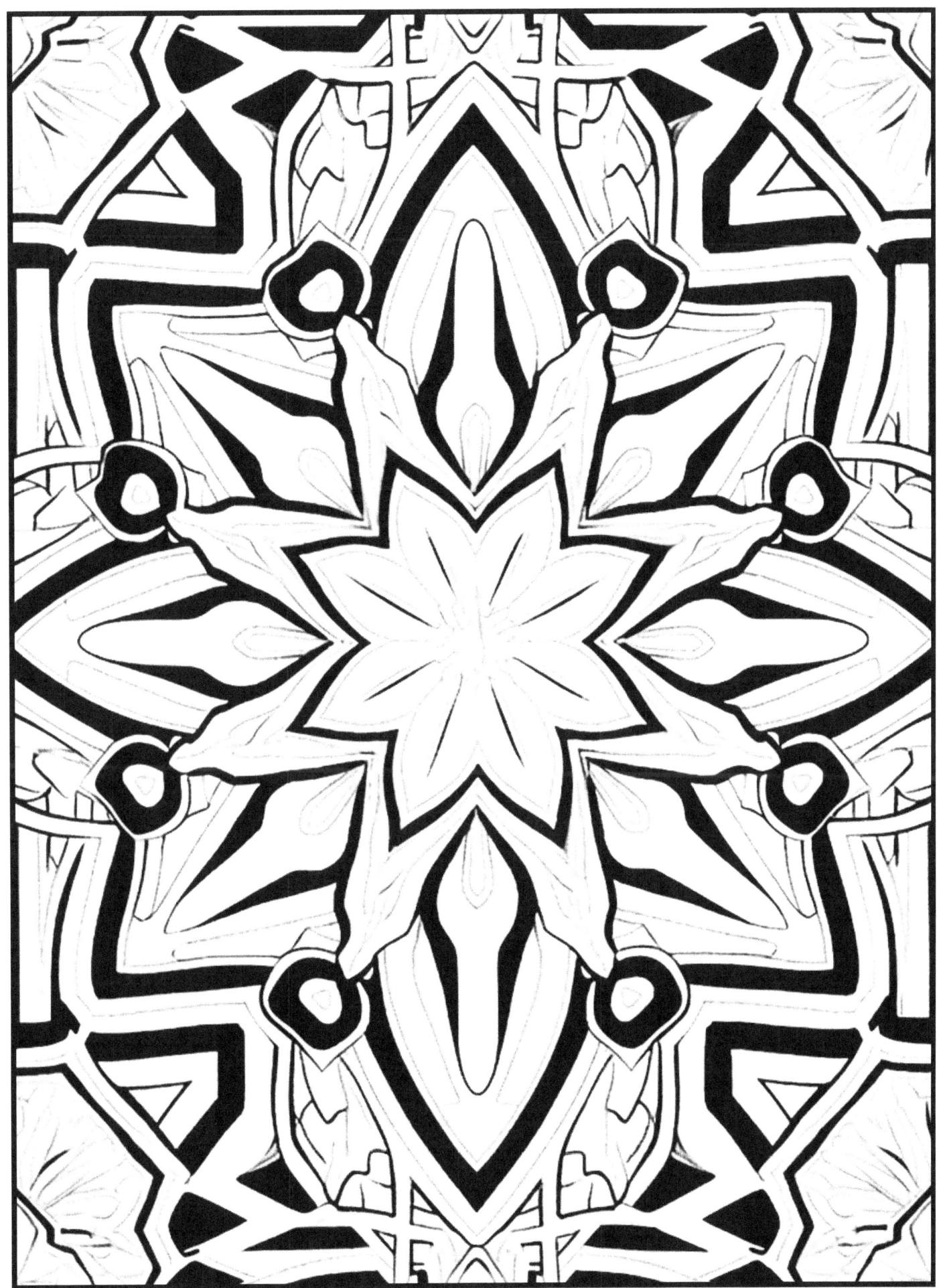

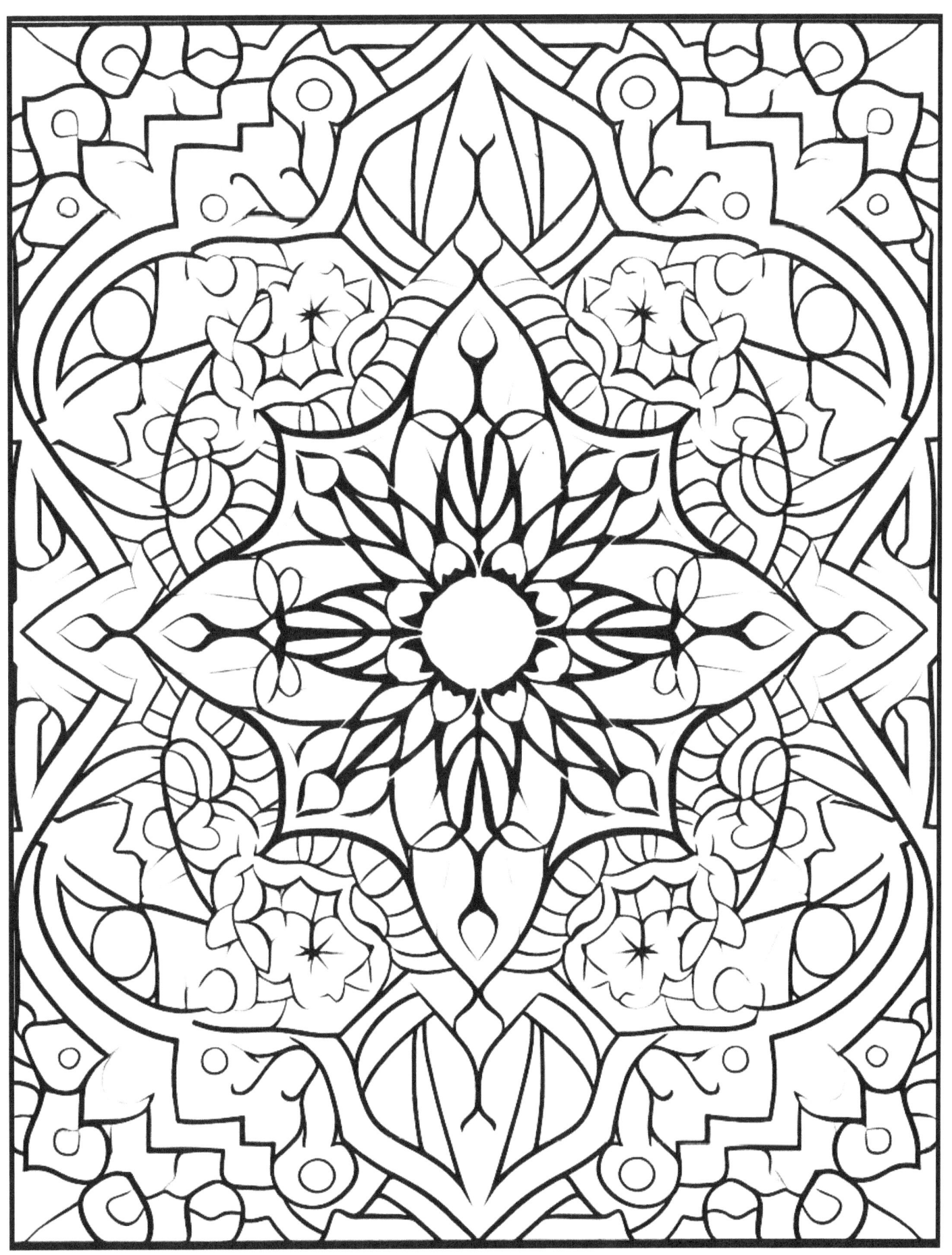

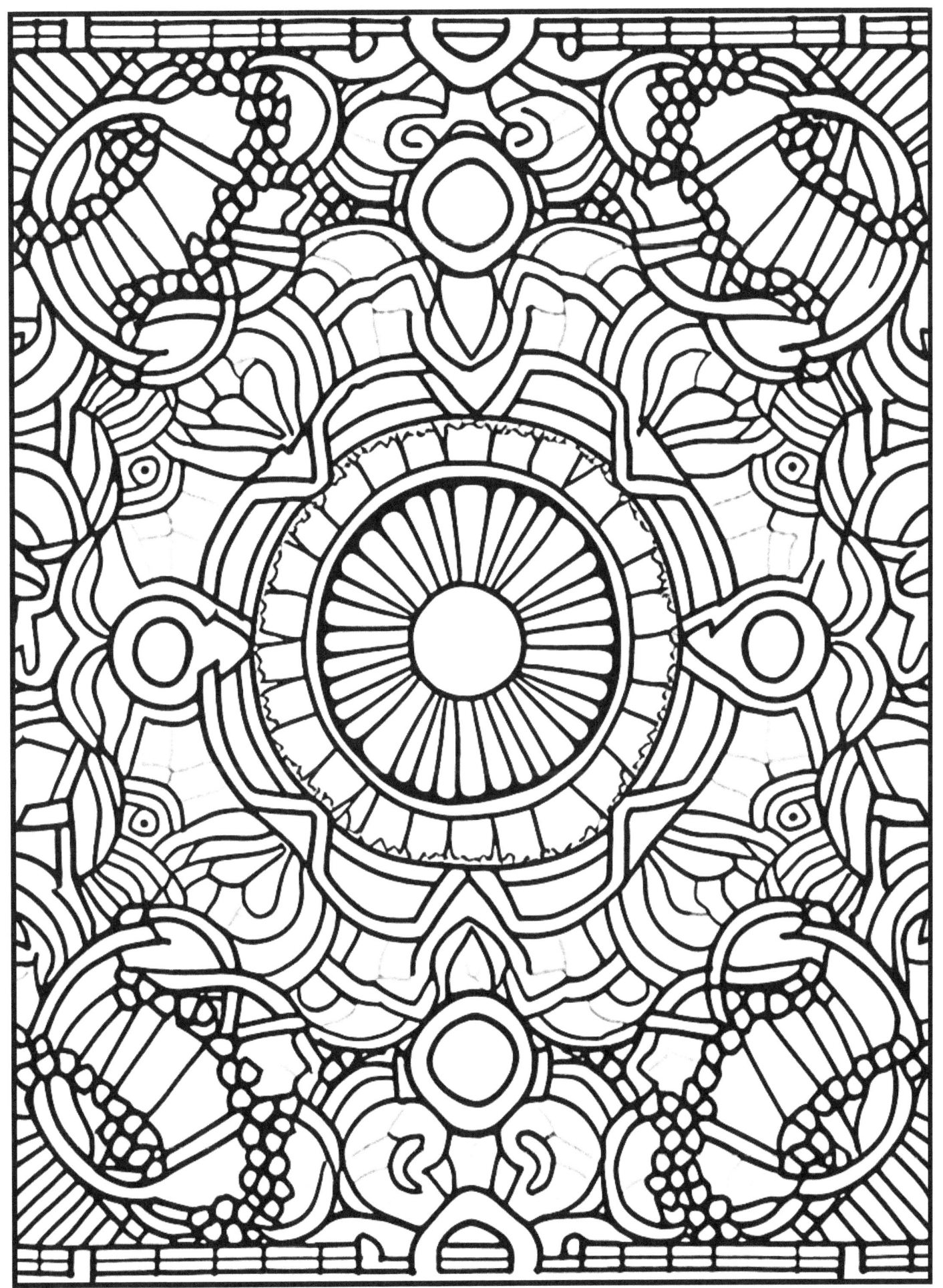

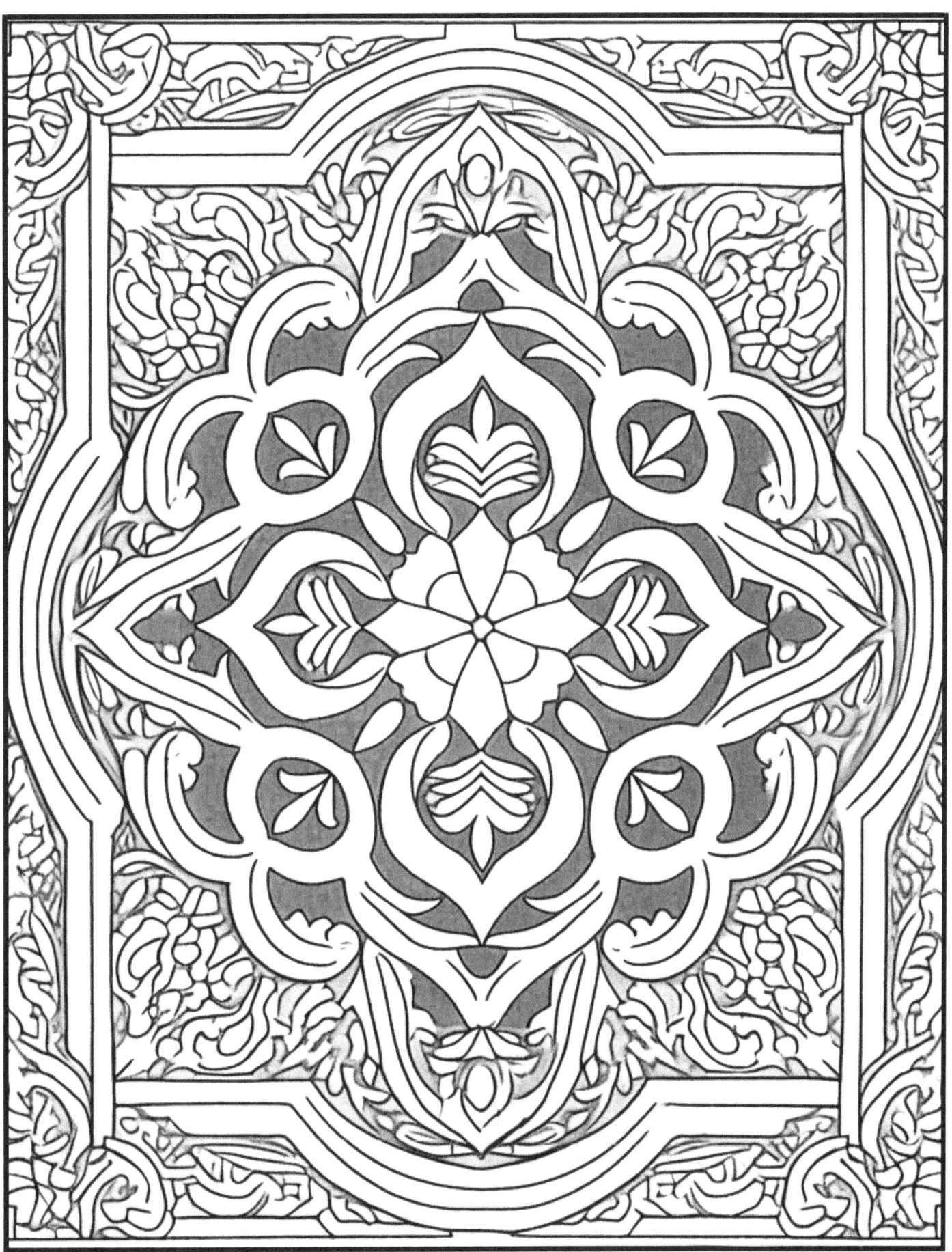

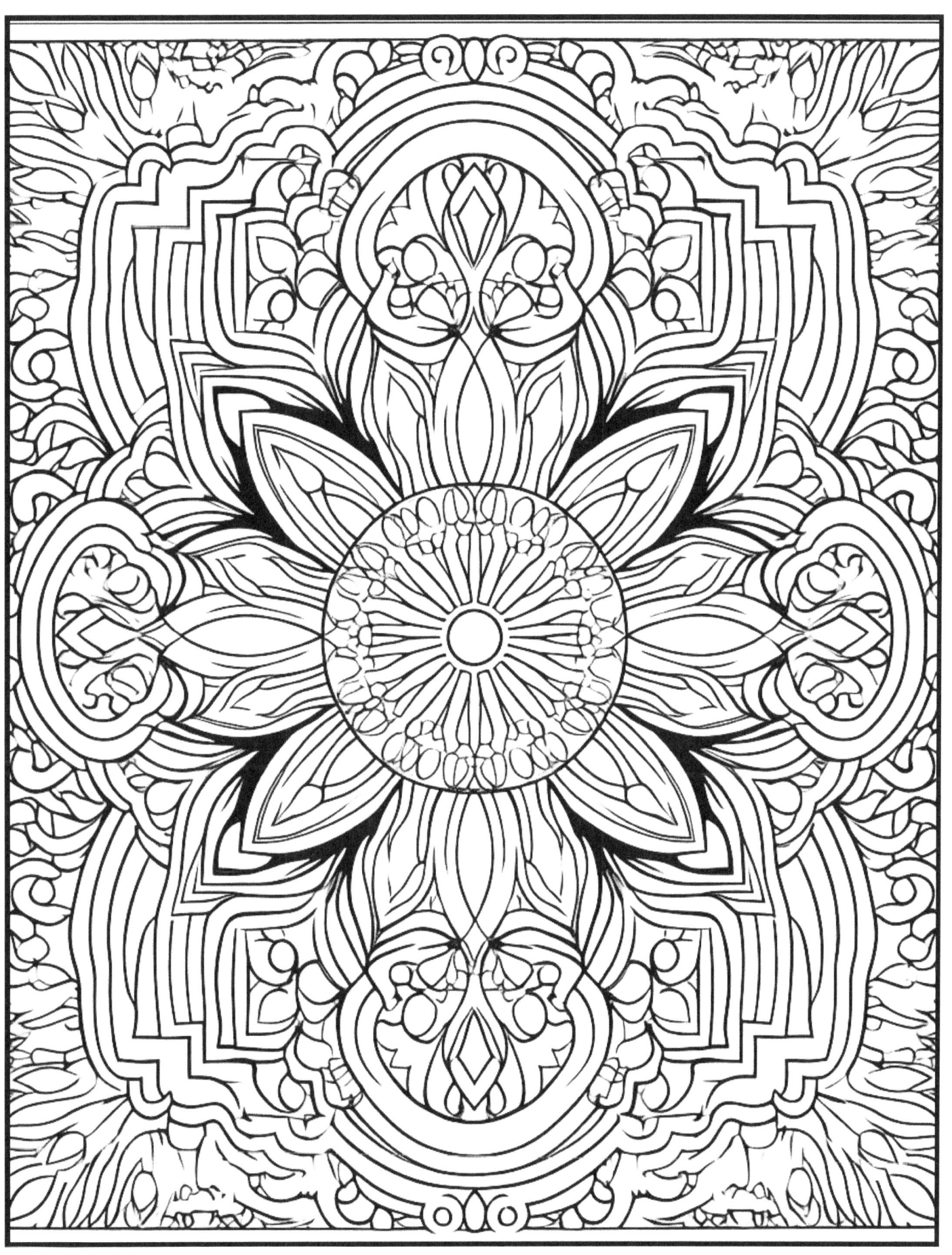

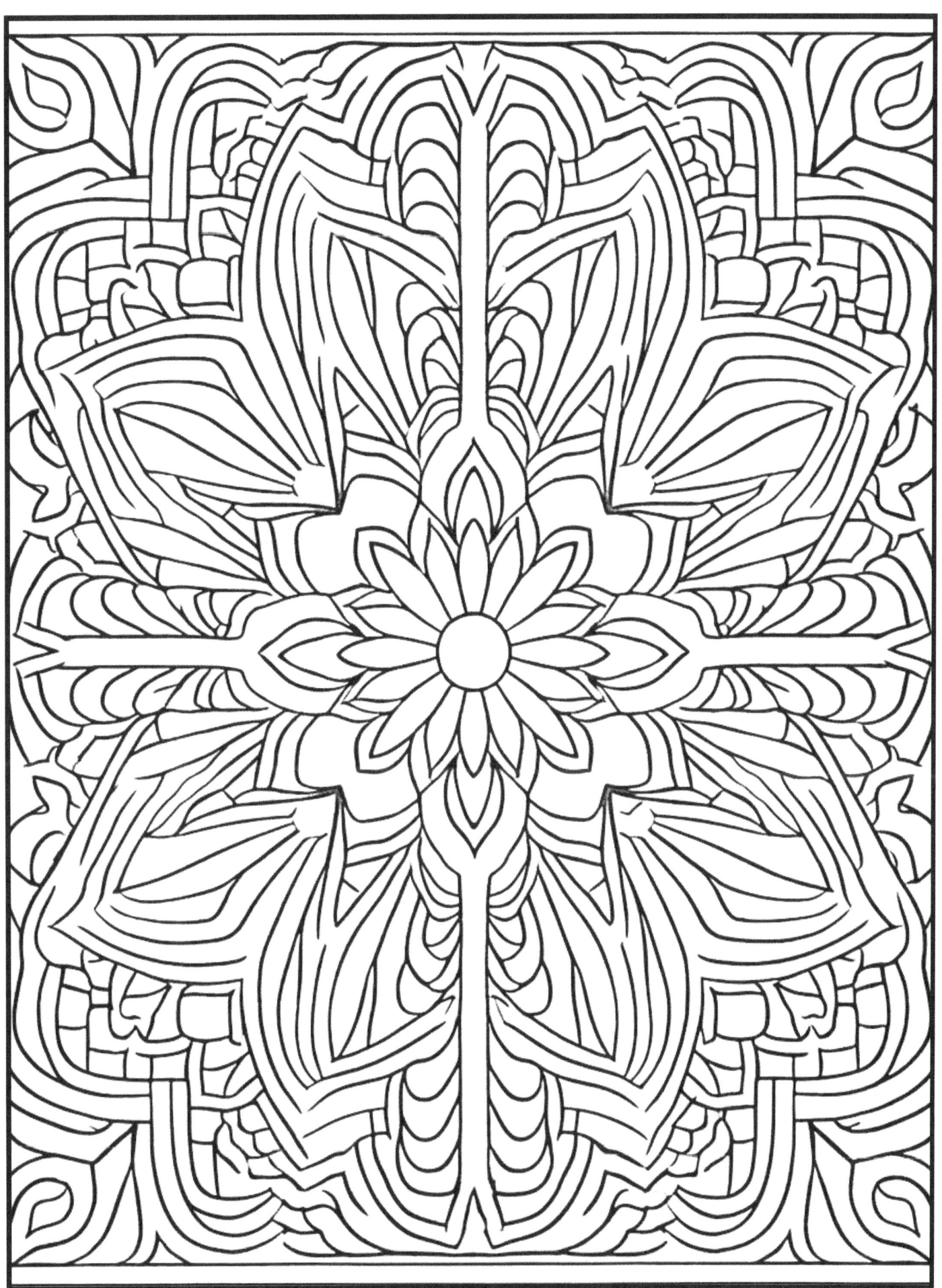